David Carr Glover
METHOD for PIANO

LESSONS

**David Carr Glover
and Jay Stewart**

D1411636

Design and Illustrations: Jeannette Aquino
Editor: Carole Flatau
Production Coordinator: Sonja Poorman

FOREWORD

Teacher and Parents:

LESSONS, Level Four, from the David Carr Glover METHOD for PIANO reviews the basic concepts presented in LESSONS, Level Three. New concepts are introduced and reinforced sequentially through the use of original compositions, folk songs and the sounds of today. This book, combined with the recommended supplementary materials, continues to assist the student in developing the ability to read and perform musically through interval recognition, sight reading and ear training.

The student will continue to experience the basic elements of improvisation as the creative activities, EXPLORE, are presented.

Supplementary materials are carefully correlated and coded with the LESSONS book to provide reinforcement of all concepts.

The David Carr Glover METHOD for PIANO has been created to provide an educational and pedagogically sound program of piano instruction.

Supplementary materials correlated with
LESSONS, Level Four, from the
David Carr Glover METHOD for PIANO

THEORY .... Introduce with Page 4

SIGHT READING AND EAR TRAINING .... Page 4

TECHNIC .... Page 6

PERFORMANCE .... Page 6

Contents

GYPSY CAMP (Solo) 4

RAGTIME JOE (Solo) 6

Sixteenth Notes and Sixteenth Rest 8

SILENT MOVIE (Solo) 9

Key of A Major, Primary Chords in A Major 10

A Major Scale and Chords 10

A Major Arpeggio, A Major Chord Inversions 10

Alberti Bass 11

ETUDE (Solo) 11

THEME from SONATA in A (Solo) [Wolfgang Amadeus Mozart] 12

SATURDAY NIGHT POLKA (Solo) 13

NIGHT TRAIN (Solo) 14

Key of E Minor, Forms of Minor Scales (Review) 16

ETUDE IN E MINOR (Solo) 17

Primary Chords in E Minor, E Harmonic Minor Scale and Chord Progression 18

E Minor Arpeggio, E Minor Chord Inversions 18

A RUSSIAN STORY (Solo) 19

THE SLOOP JOHN B. (Solo) 20

THE GOOD OLD DAYS OF ROCK AND ROLL (Solo) 22

SPACE ENCOUNTERS (Solo) 24

Grace Note 25

MINUET IN C (Solo) 25

COME LET US TO THE BAGPIPE'S SOUND (Solo) [J.S. Bach] 26

Dotted Eighth Note 28

A CLASSICAL DANCE (Solo) 28

Key Of Bb Major, Primary Chords in Bb Major 30

Bb Major Scale and Chords 30

Bb Major Arpeggio, Bb Major Chord Inversions 30

Alla Breve 31

GOOD NIGHT LADIES! (Solo) 31

THE BATTLE HYMN OF THE REPUBLIC (Solo) 32

Key of G Minor, G Minor Natural-Harmonic-Melodic Scales 34

Primary Chords in G Minor, G Harmonic Minor Scale and Chords 34

G Minor Arpeggio, G Minor Chord Inversions 34

SPOOK HOUSE (Solo) 35

HAVAH NAGILAH (Solo) 36

Key of Eb Major, Primary Chords in Eb Major 38

Eb Major Scale and Chords 38

Eb Major Arpeggio, Eb Major Chord Inversions 38

AMAZING GRACE (Solo) 39

Slight Accent Mark 40

SPANISH NIGHTS (Solo) 40

Key of C Minor, C Minor Natural-Harmonic-Melodic Scales 42

Primary Chords in C Minor, C Harmonic Minor Scale and Chords 42

C Minor Arpeggio, C Minor Chord Inversions 42

THE SASSY CAMEL (Solo) 43

SOLFEGGIETTO (Solo) 44

Augmented Triads 46

WIDE RIVER (Solo) 46

Diminished Triads 48

PIRATE'S QUAY (Solo) 48

Circle of Keys 50

Scale and Chord Dictionary 51

Review 57

Music Dictionary 58

Certificate 60

GYPSY CAMP

A Minor Review

STEWART

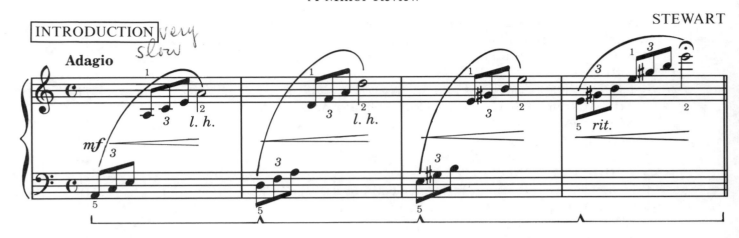

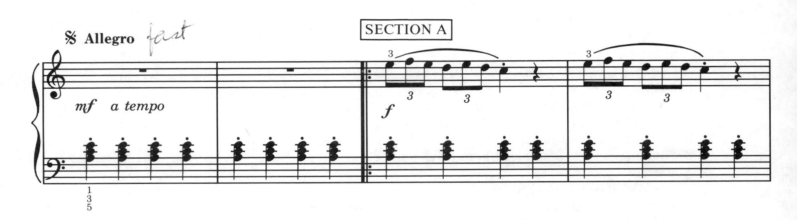

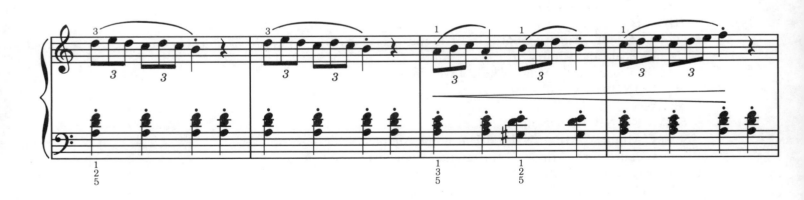

SECTION B

D. S. al ✛ , then to Coda

CODA

espressivo: with expression

You are now ready for Level Four THEORY and
Level Four SIGHT READING AND EAR TRAINING
from the David Carr Glover METHOD for PIANO.

RAGTIME JOE

Syncopation Review

GLOVER - STEWART

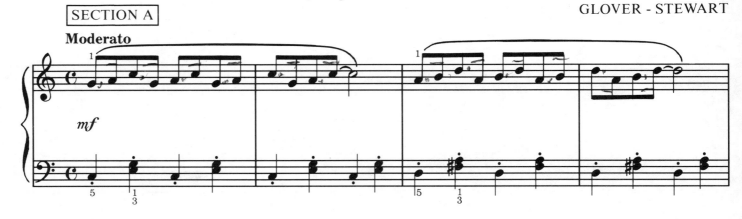

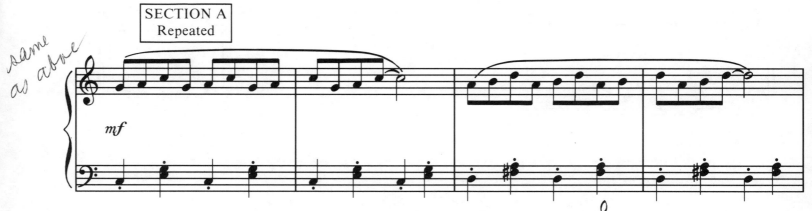

EXPLORE: Tap the rhythm of this piece hands together (right hand taps 𝄞 and left hand taps 𝄢) as you count aloud. Do this activity for other solos in this book.

You are now ready for Level Four TECHNIC and
Level Four PERFORMANCE
from the David Carr Glover METHOD for PIANO.

Sixteenth Notes and Sixteenth Rest

A single sixteenth note has two flags.

A sixteenth rest has two flags.

Two or more sixteenth notes may be connected by a double beam.

When the quarter note receives one beat, the sixteenth note receives one-fourth beat.

Four sixteenth notes are equal in time value to one quarter note in $\frac{2}{4}$, $\frac{3}{4}$ or $\frac{4}{4}$ time.

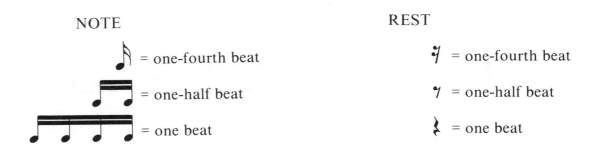

NOTE		REST	
	= one-fourth beat		= one-fourth beat
	= one-half beat		= one-half beat
	= one beat		= one beat

1. Clap and count this rhythm aloud.

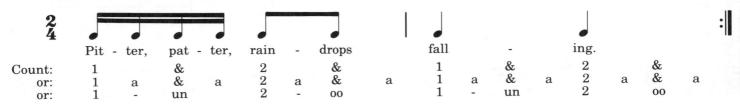

Pit -	ter,	pat -	ter,	rain -	drops	fall	-	ing.			
Count:	1		&	2	&	1	&	2	&		
or:	1	a	&	a 2	a &	a 1	a &	a 2	a &	a	
or:	1	-	un	2	- oo	1	- un	2	oo		

Your teacher will tell you which way to count.

2. Count aloud as you play.

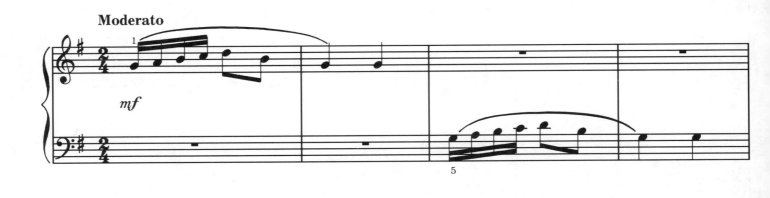

SILENT MOVIE

D Minor Review

STEWART

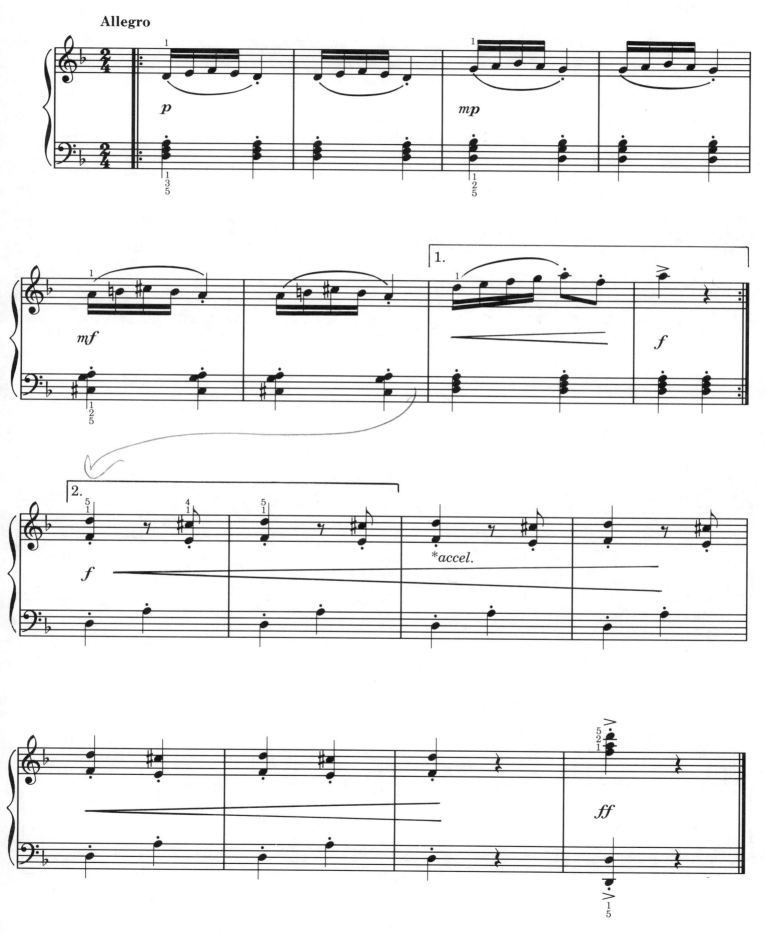

* *accelerando:* gradually quicker

10

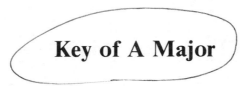

Key of A Major

Primary Chords in A Major

A Major Scale and Chords

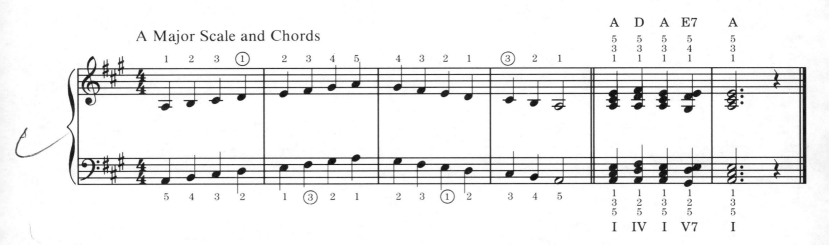

A Major Arpeggio
Stems up - *r.h.*
Stems down - *l.h.*

A Major Chord Inversions

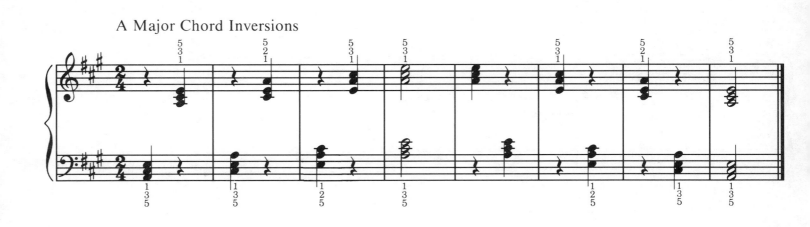

ALBERTI BASS is an accompaniment form that consists of broken chords played in this style:

The Alberti Bass is named after the Italian composer Domenico Alberti (c. 1710-1740), who used it frequently in his harpsichord sonatas.

ETUDE

GLOVER

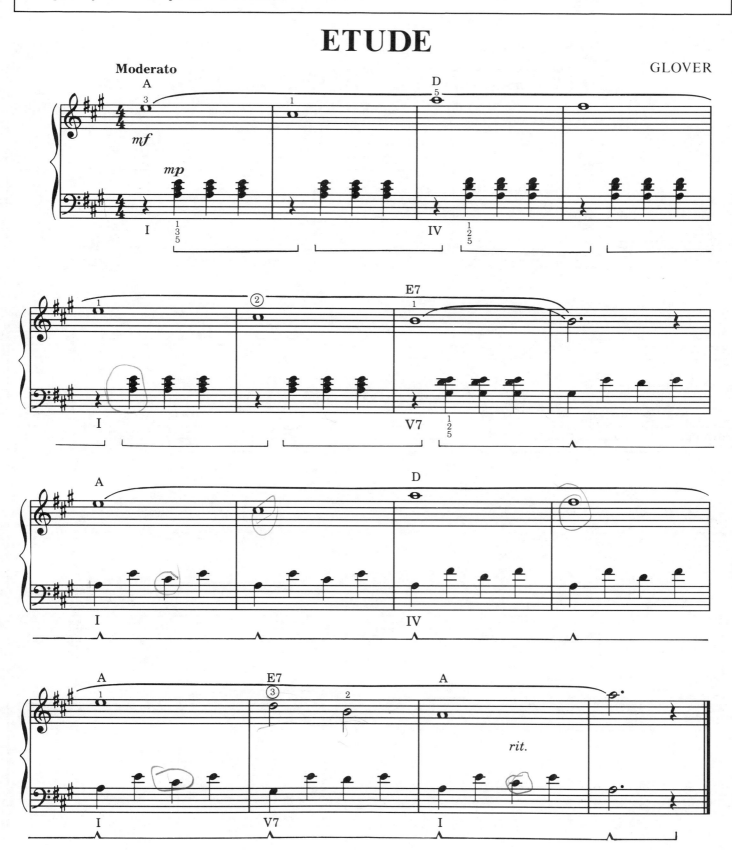

EXPLORE: Play this piece using an Alberti Bass left hand accompaniment throughout.

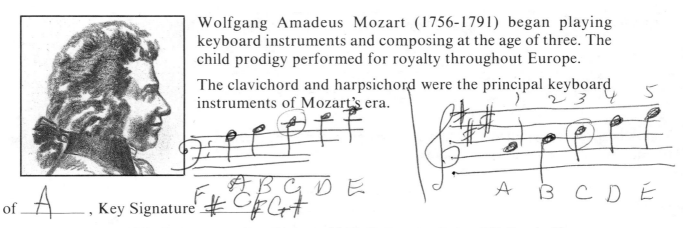

Wolfgang Amadeus Mozart (1756-1791) began playing keyboard instruments and composing at the age of three. The child prodigy performed for royalty throughout Europe.

The clavichord and harpsichord were the principal keyboard instruments of Mozart's era.

Key of ___A___ , Key Signature ___#___

THEME FROM "SONATA IN A"
* (adapted)

MOZART

* TEACHER: The Glover-Stewart arrangements of the classics have been carefully planned so they will provide an accurate foundation for later study of the original works.

SATURDAY NIGHT POLKA

1st Inversion Triad Review

STEWART

EXPLORE: Play measures 1 through 12 one octave lower.

NIGHT TRAIN

1st Inversion Triad Review

Moderately slow

GLOVER - STEWART

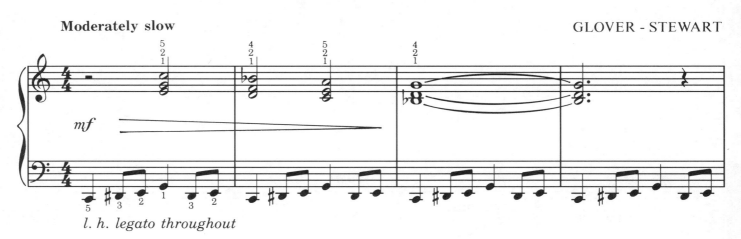

l. h. legato throughout

EXPLORE: Compose your own Blues piece in **4/4** time, C Major. Play the following progression with your left hand using whole note blocked chords, as you create a right hand melody.

C / C / C / C
F / F / C / C
G / F / C / C

Key of E Minor

Each major key has a RELATIVE MINOR key with the SAME KEY SIGNATURE. The relative minor scale begins on the 6th tone of the related major scale. The two scales are related because they share the same key signature.

G MAJOR SCALE

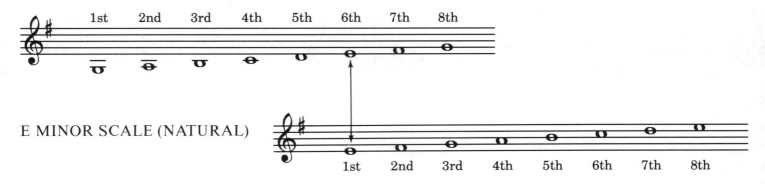

E MINOR SCALE (NATURAL)

Forms of Minor Scales (Review)

There are several kinds of Minor Scales. Three are presented below:
(1) the NATURAL, (2) the HARMONIC, (3) the MELODIC.

Practice these scales. Play the right hand as written. Play the left hand one octave lower than written. Use correct fingering.

1. The NATURAL MINOR SCALE uses the same tones as the relative major scale.

2. The HARMONIC MINOR SCALE uses the same tones as the NATURAL MINOR SCALE with the exception of the 7th tone which is raised one half step. This raised 7th tone is not included in the key signature.

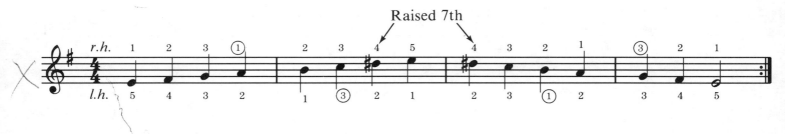

3. The MELODIC MINOR SCALE uses the same tones as the NATURAL MINOR SCALE with the exception of the 6th and 7th tones which are raised one half step ASCENDING, then lowered DESCENDING.

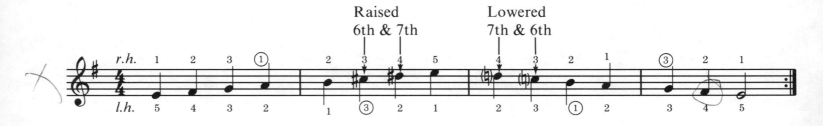

Which form of the E minor scale is used in this Etude? _____

ETUDE IN E MINOR

GLOVER

Primary Chords in E Minor

Primary chords in a minor key are formed by using the notes of the HARMONIC MINOR SCALE. The 7th tone of the scale is raised one half step.

Lower case Roman numerals are used to indicate the minor triads (i, iv).
Lower case **m** after the chord letter name indicates a minor chord (Em = E minor).

In minor keys the i and iv chords are minor chords.
The V7 chord is always a major chord.
Minor chords, like major chords, can be inverted.

Practice the following E Harmonic Minor Scale, chord progression, arpeggio and chord inversions.

Use correct fingering.

E Harmonic Minor Scale and Chord Progression

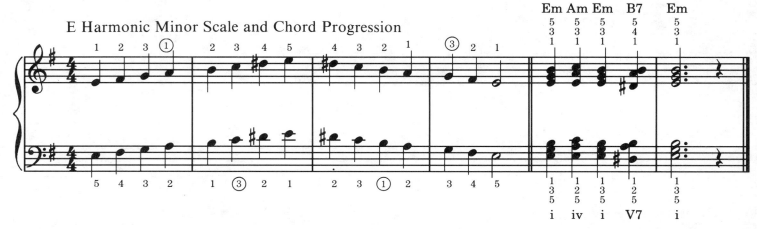

E Minor Arpeggio

Stems up - *r.h.*
Stems down - *l.h.*

E Minor Chord Inversions

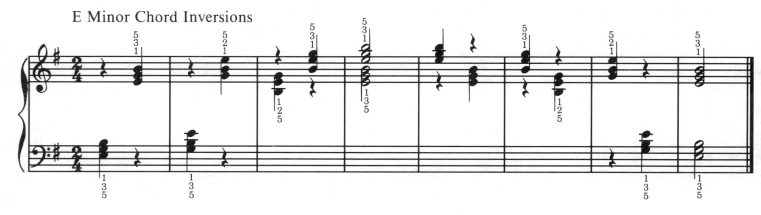

Key of _____ , Key Signature _____

A RUSSIAN STORY

GLOVER - STEWART

THE SLOOP JOHN B.

2nd Inversion Triad Review

FOLK TUNE

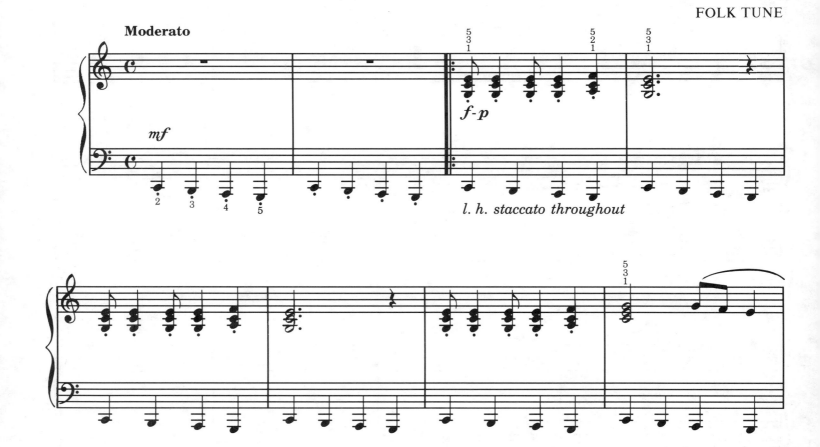

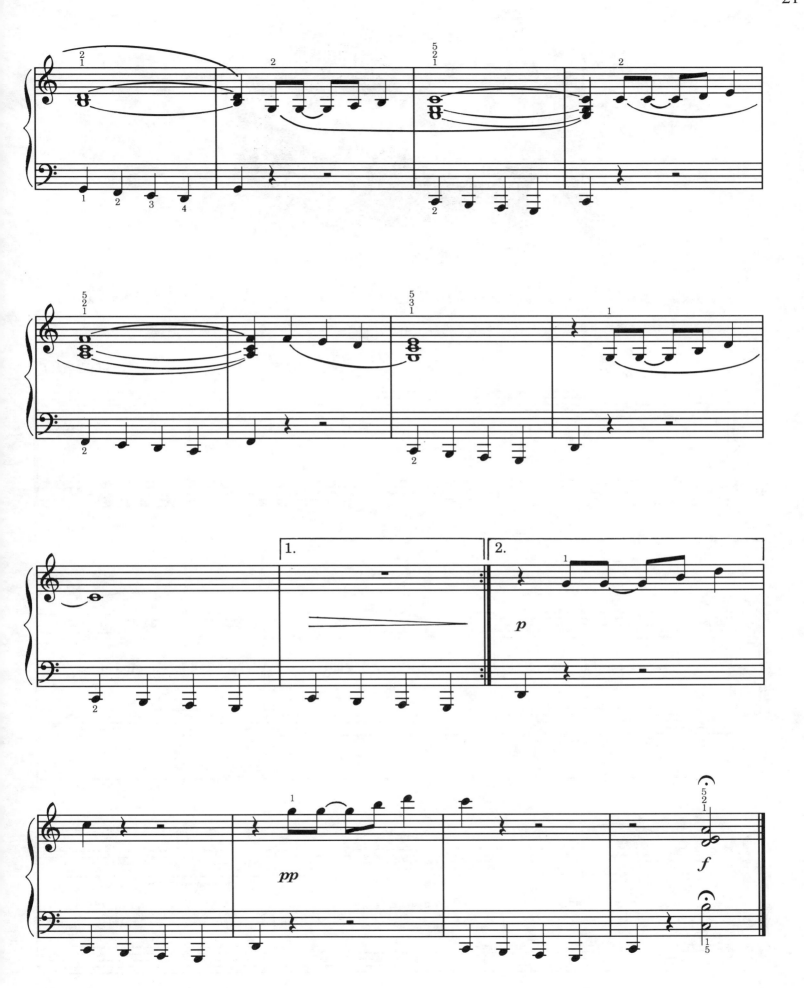

EXPLORE: Tap the rhythm of this piece (right hand and left hand together) as you count aloud. Do this
activity with several other pieces in this book.

THE GOOD OLD DAYS OF ROCK AND ROLL

2nd Inversion Triad Review

STEWART

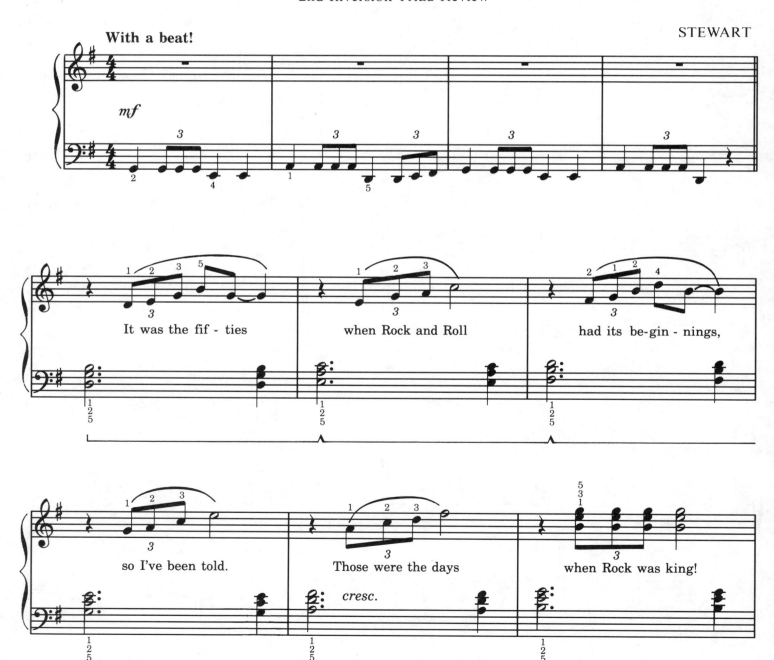

It was the fif - ties   when Rock and Roll   had its be-gin - nings,

so I've been told.   Those were the days   when Rock was king!

SPACE ENCOUNTERS

1st and 2nd Inversion Triads

GLOVER - STEWART

GRACE NOTE

The GRACE NOTE is written as a small eighth note and usually has a line drawn through it.

The grace note has no time value and is not counted as part of the rhythm.
Play the grace note very quickly before the principal note.

MINUET IN C

STEWART

delicate
elegant

SECTION A

Moderato

mf

mp

l. h. legato

mp

rit. 2nd time

1. *To Next Strain*   2.

Fine

SECTION B

f

p

D. C. al Fine
(with 2nd ending)

Johann Sebastian Bach (1685-1750) was born in Eisenach, Saxe-Weimar, Germany. He is considered one of the greatest composers. He wrote hundreds of compositions, many of them for his children and pupils. He was also a famous organist and wrote many church cantatas and oratorios.

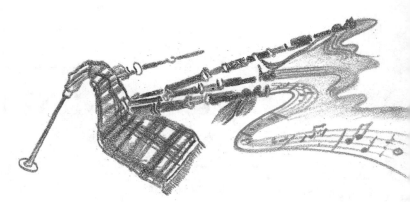

Baroque

COME LET US TO THE BAGPIPE'S SOUND

from "The Peasant Cantata"
Adapted

J.S. BACH

F Key

SECTION A

Allegro

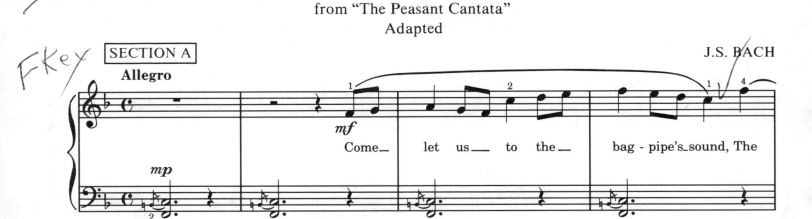

Come— let us— to the— bag - pipe's sound, The

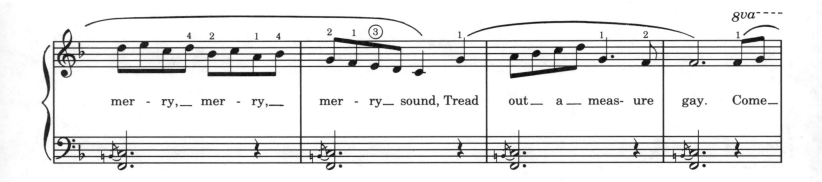

mer - ry,— mer - ry,— mer - ry— sound, Tread out— a— meas- ure gay. Come—

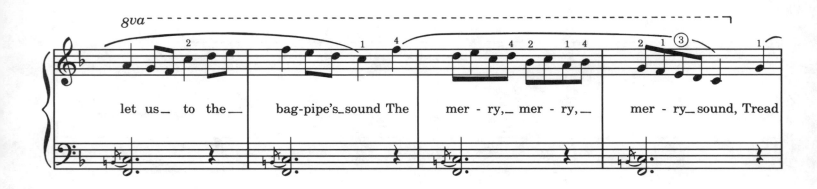

let us— to the— bag-pipe's sound The mer - ry,— mer - ry,— mer - ry— sound, Tread

SECTION B

SECTION A

Dotted Eighth Note

The DOTTED EIGHTH NOTE is equal in value to three sixteenth notes.

It is usually followed by a sixteenth note.

The two notes are equal to one quarter note.

1. Clap and count aloud.

A CLASSICAL DANCE

SECTION A

GLOVER

Key of B♭ Major

Primary Chords in B♭ Major

B♭ Major Scale and Chords

B♭ Major Arpeggio
Stems up - *r.h.*
Stems down - *l.h.*

B♭ Major Chord Inversions

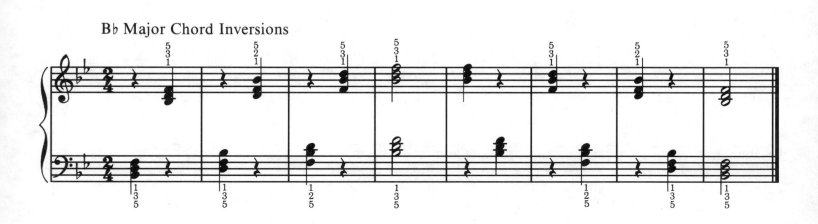

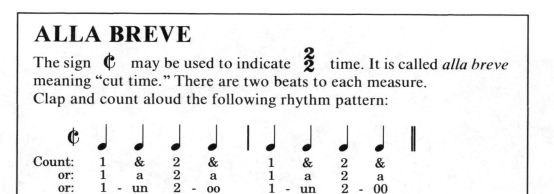

ALLA BREVE

The sign $\mathbb{C}$ may be used to indicate $\frac{2}{2}$ time. It is called *alla breve* meaning "cut time." There are two beats to each measure.
Clap and count aloud the following rhythm pattern:

Count:	1	&	2	&	1	&	2	&
or:	1	a	2	a	1	a	2	a
or:	1 - un	2 - oo	1 - un	2 - 00

Your teacher will tell you which way to count.

GOOD NIGHT LADIES!

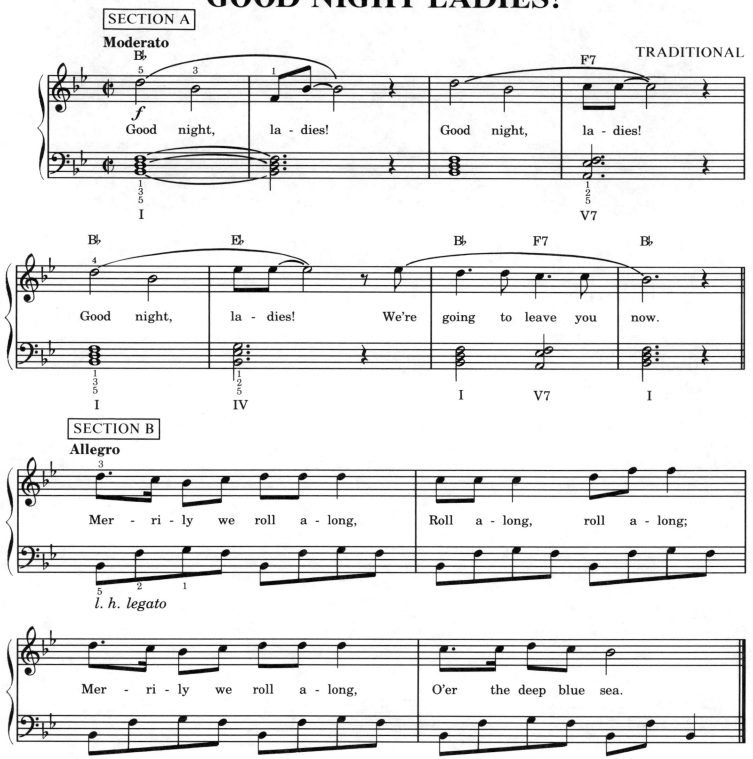

THE BATTLE HYMN OF THE REPUBLIC

Key of _Bb maj_ Key Signature _Bb Eb_

STEFFE-HOWE

INTRODUCTION

Left hand plays a cluster of the five lowest white keys on the keyboard.

SECTION A

SECTION B

* *poco a poco:* little by little

Key of G Minor

G Natural Minor Scale

(Play *l.h.* one octave lower than written.)

G Harmonic Minor Scale

G Melodic Minor Scale

Primary Chords in G Minor

G Harmonic Minor Scale and Chords

G Minor Arpeggio

Stems up - *r.h.*
Stems down - *l.h.*

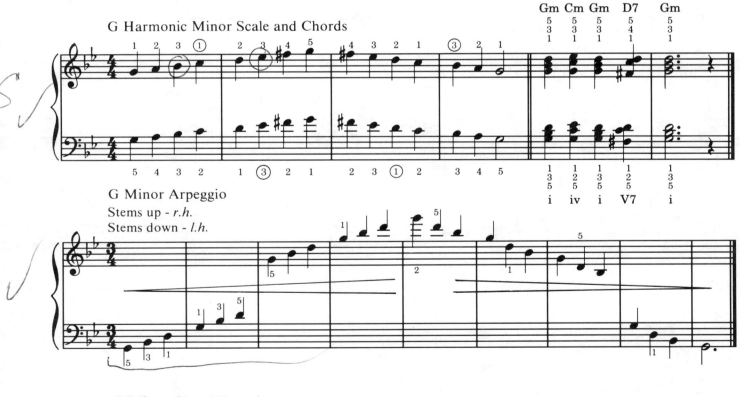

G Minor Chord Inversions

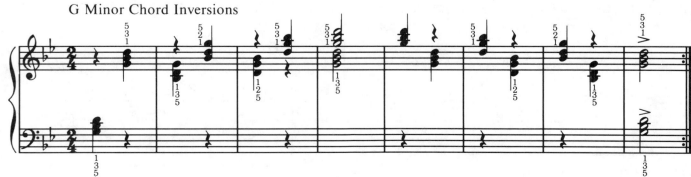

SPOOK HOUSE

GLOVER - STEWART

SECTION A

Presto (very fast)

SECTION B

CODA

EXPLORE: Transpose this piece to the key of G Major.

HAVAH NAGILAH

ISRAELI FOLK TUNE

Moderato

EXPLORE: Repeat as many times as desired from measure 5, each time faster than before, until dancers could not continue. (Dancers often dance until they fall down!)

Key of E♭ Major

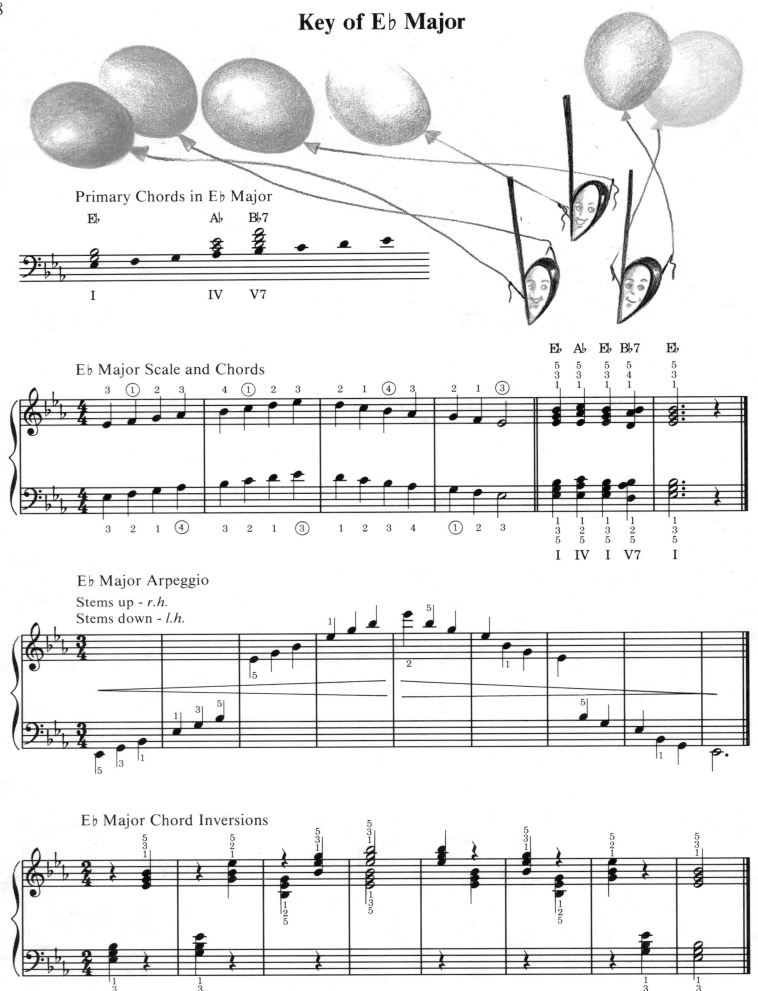

Primary Chords in E♭ Major

E♭ Major Scale and Chords

E♭ Major Arpeggio

Stems up - *r.h.*
Stems down - *l.h.*

E♭ Major Chord Inversions

TEACHER: See pages 51-56 for major and relative minor scales and chords in all keys.

AMAZING GRACE

TRADITIONAL

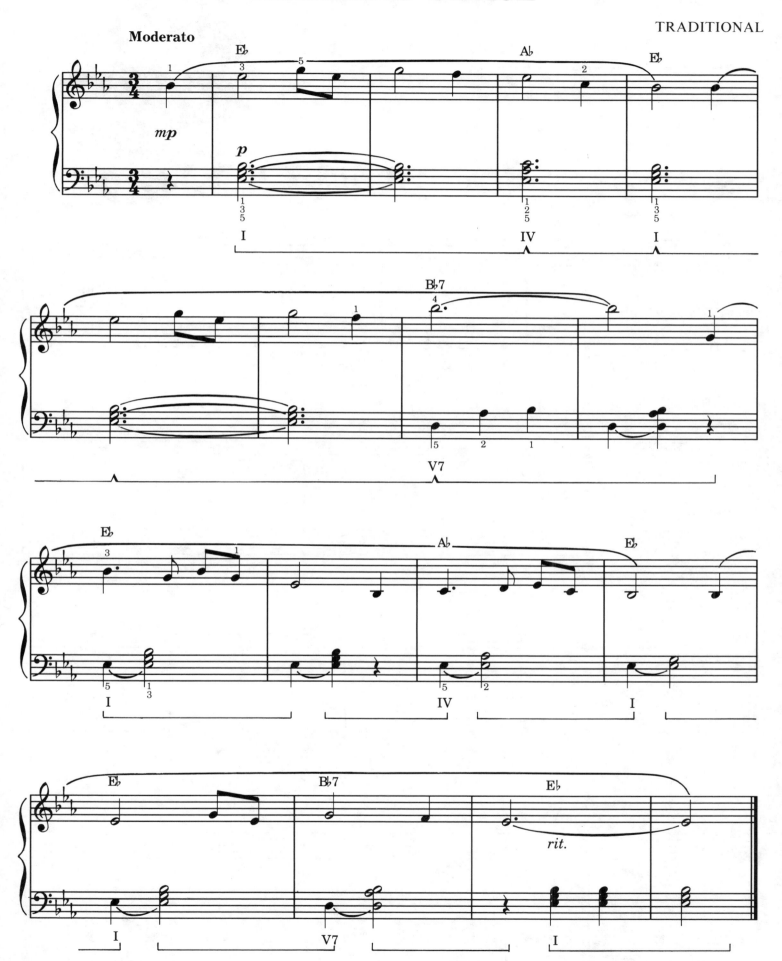

EXPLORE: Repeat this solo as follows. First eight measures: play the left hand one octave higher; play
the right hand two octaves lower (over the left hand). Last eight measures: play as written.

SLIGHT ACCENT MARK

When this accent mark — is used above or below a note,
the note is slightly accented with a sustained quality.

Key of _____ , Key Signature _____

Observe the changes of time signatures
and tempo marks.

SPANISH NIGHTS

STEWART

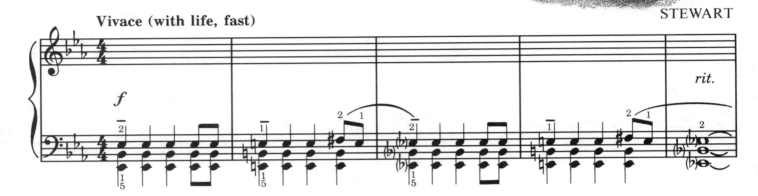

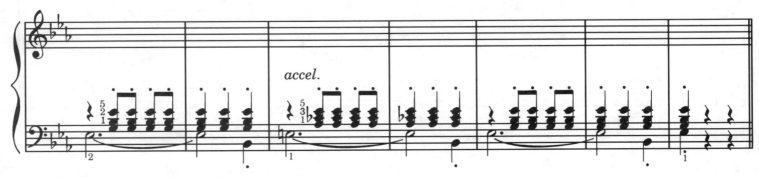

* *Cantabile:* in a singing style

Key of C Minor

C Natural Minor Scale
Play *l.h.* one octave lower than written.

C Harmonic Minor Scale

C Melodic Minor Scale

Primary Chords in C Minor

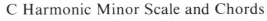

C Harmonic Minor Scale and Chords

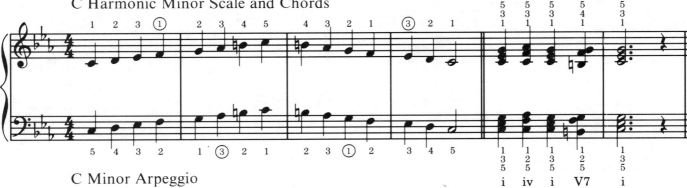

C Minor Arpeggio
Stems up - *r.h.*
Stems down - *l.h.*

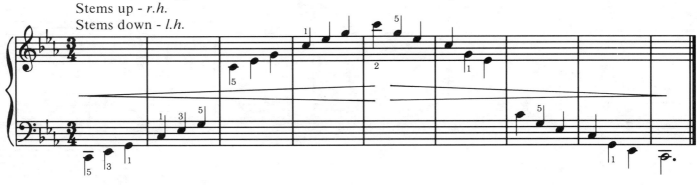

C Minor Chord Inversions

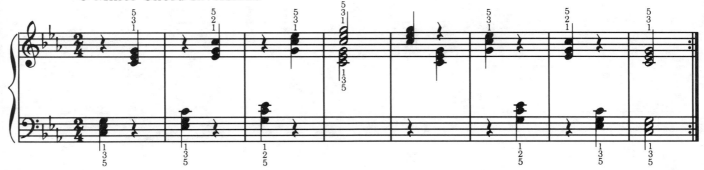

THE SASSY CAMEL

STEWART

EXPLORE: Tap the rhythm of this piece, hands together, as you count aloud. Right hand taps and left hand taps 𝄢

Key of _____ , Key Signature _____

SOLFEGGIETTO
(Little Study)

STEWART

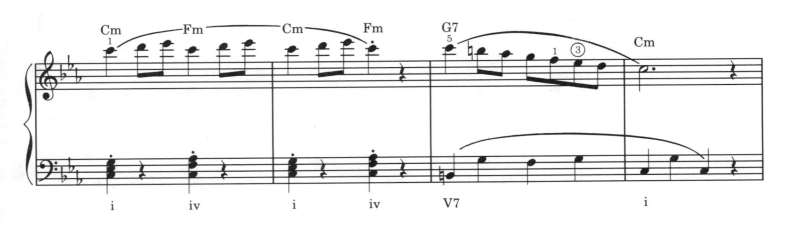

Augmented Triads

AUGMENT means to make larger.
A major triad becomes an augmented (larger) triad when the top note (the 5th) is raised one half step.

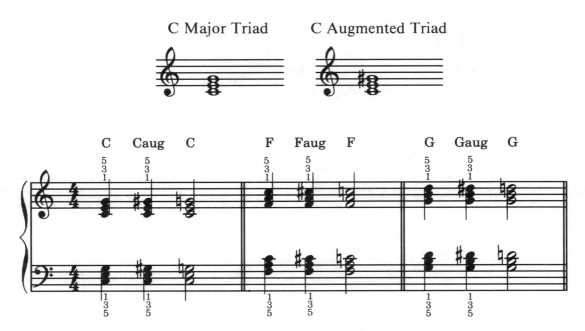

An augmented chord may also be indicated with a + sign.

WIDE RIVER

GLOVER - STEWART

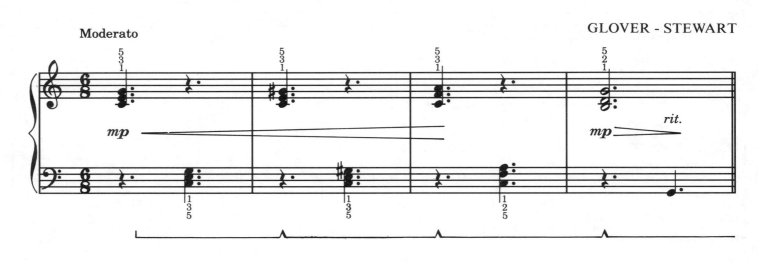

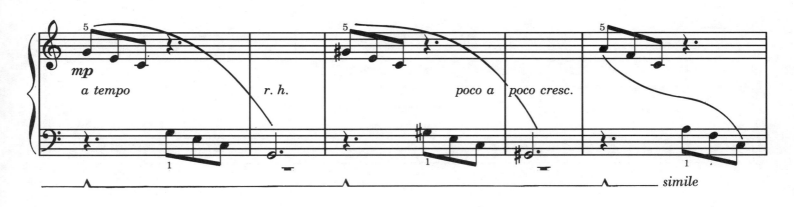

Diminished Triads

DIMINISH means to make smaller.
A minor triad becomes a diminished (smaller) triad when the top note (the 5th) is lowered one half step.

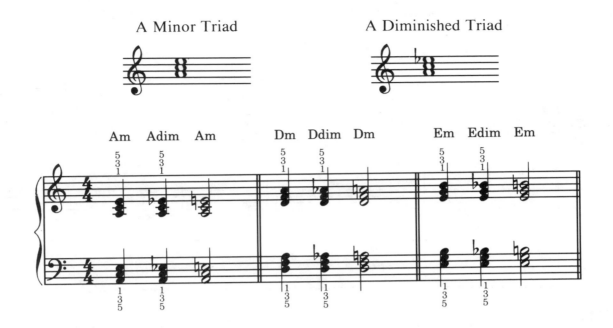

A diminished chord may also be indicated with a ° sign.

PIRATE'S QUAY*

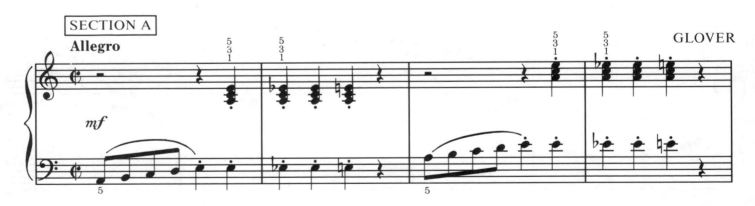

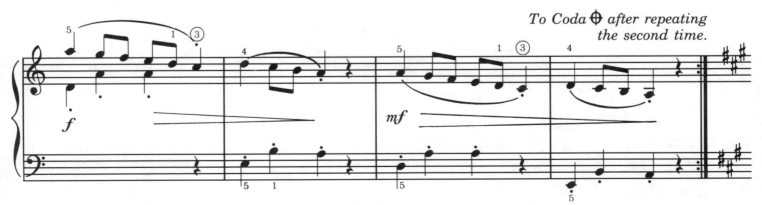

* Quay (Key): a place where ships are loaded and unloaded.

Circle of Keys

This CIRCLE OF KEYS shows the key signature of all major and relative minor keys.

Begin at the top and move clockwise to find the sharp key signatures.

Move counterclockwise from the top to find the flat key signatures.

Notice that the sharp keys progress at intervals of a 5th around the circle.
The flat keys progress at intervals of a 4th around the circle.

Keys with two names are called ENHARMONIC (such as C♯ Major and D♭ Major,
F♯ Major and G♭ Major, B Major and C♭ Major and their relative minor keys).

The enharmonic keys are located at the bottom of this CIRCLE OF KEYS.

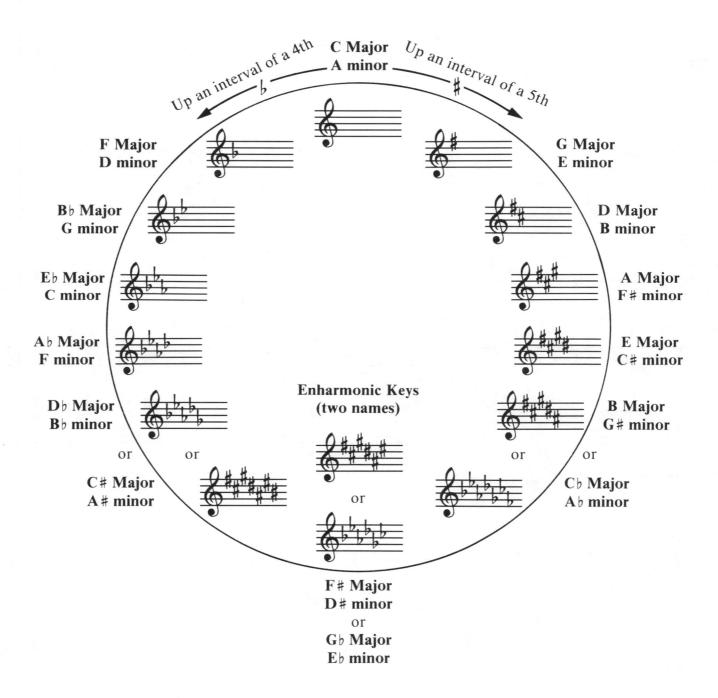

Scale and Chord Dictionary

C Major

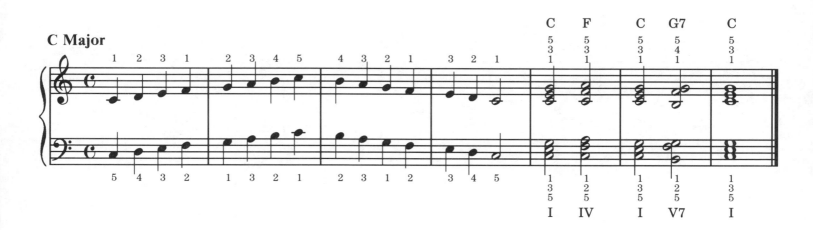

A Harmonic minor (relative to C Major)

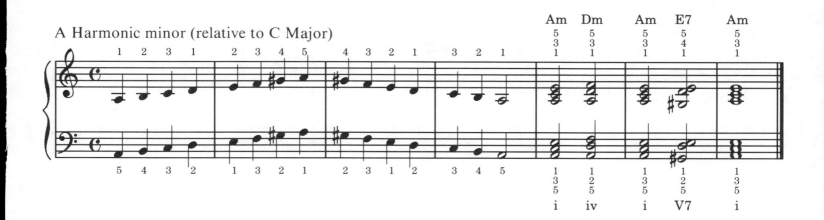

G Major

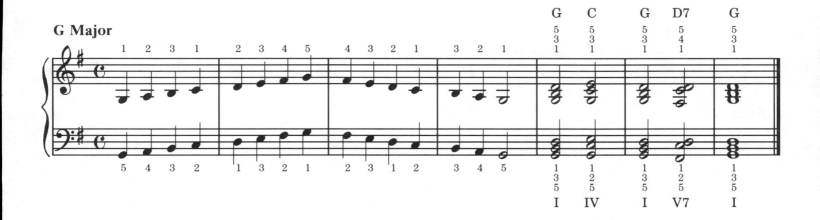

E Harmonic minor (relative to G Major)

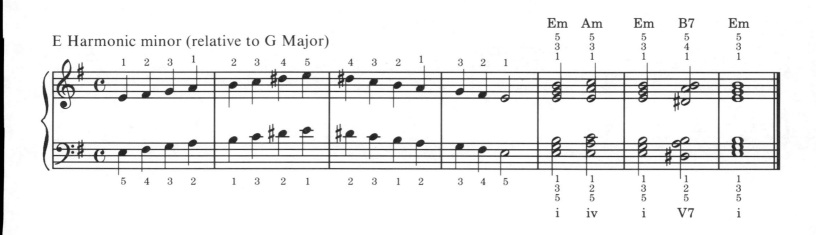

52

D Major

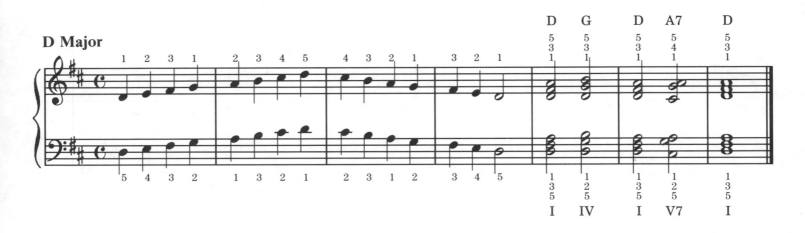

B Harmonic minor (relative to D Major)

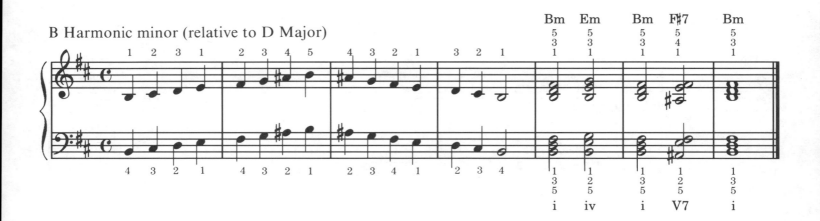

A Major

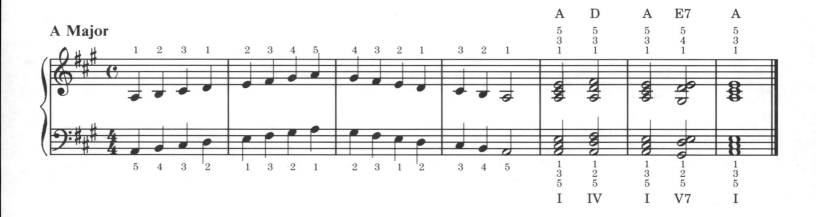

F♯ Harmonic minor (relative to A Major)

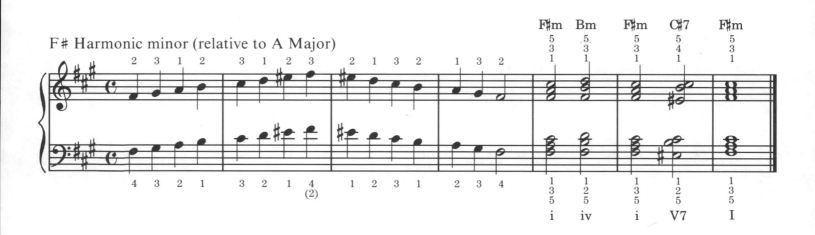

(2)

E Major

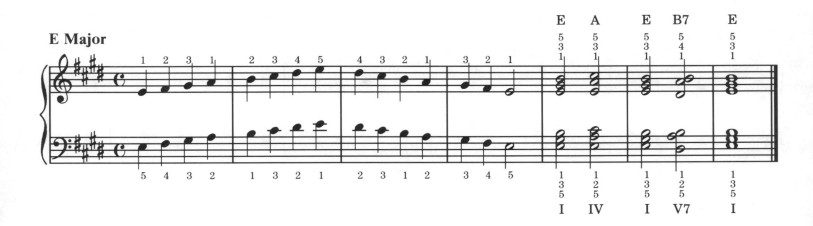

C♯ Harmonic minor (relative to E Major)

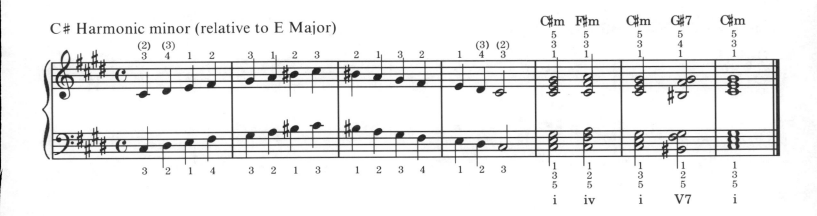

B Major

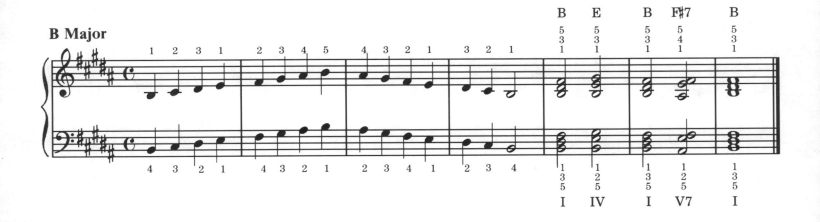

G♯ Harmonic minor (relative to B Major)

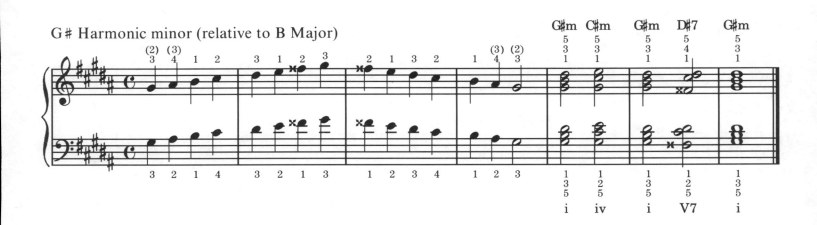

F Major

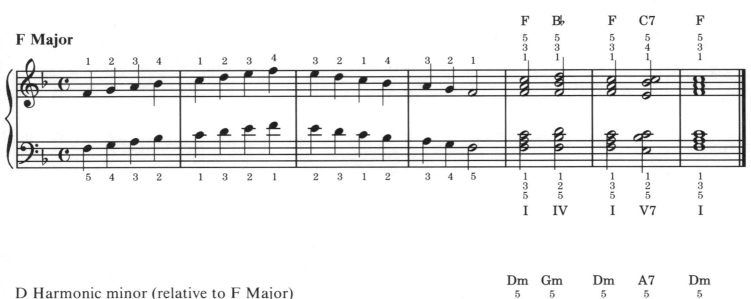

D Harmonic minor (relative to F Major)

B♭ Major

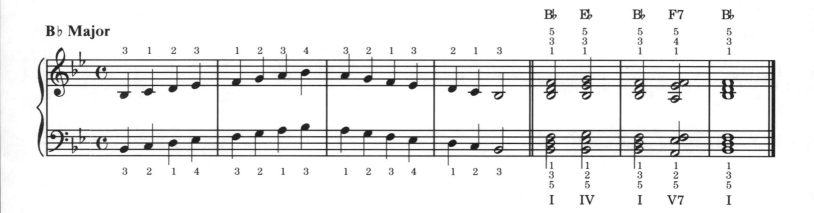

G Harmonic minor (relative to B♭ Major)

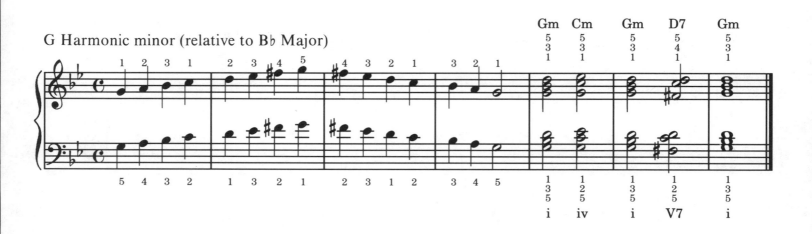

E♭ Major

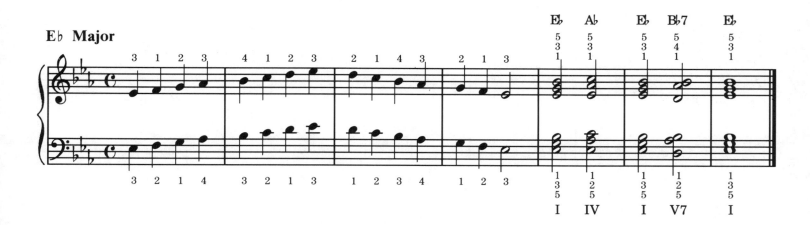

C Harmonic minor (relative to E♭ Major)

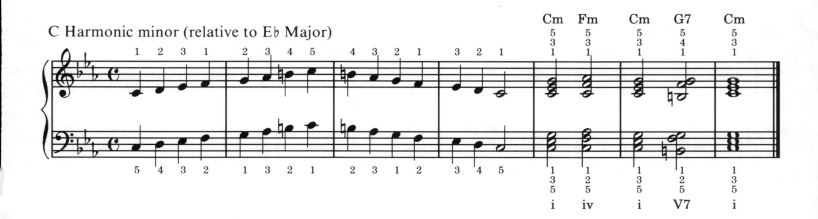

A♭ Major

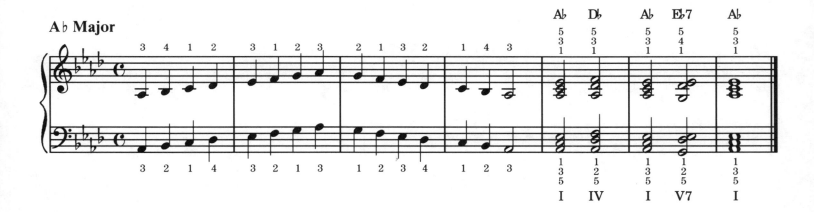

F Harmonic minor (relative to A♭ Major)

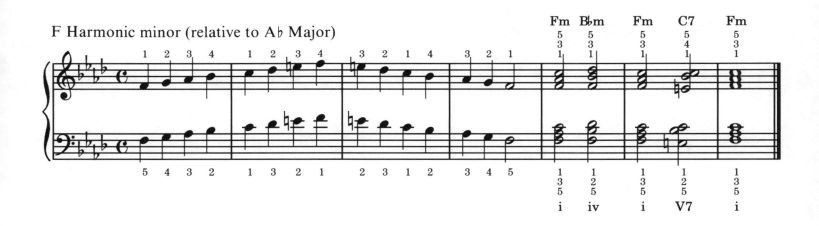

D♭ Major

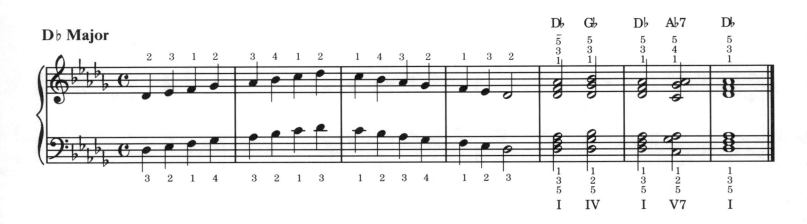

B♭ Harmonic minor (relative to D♭ Major)

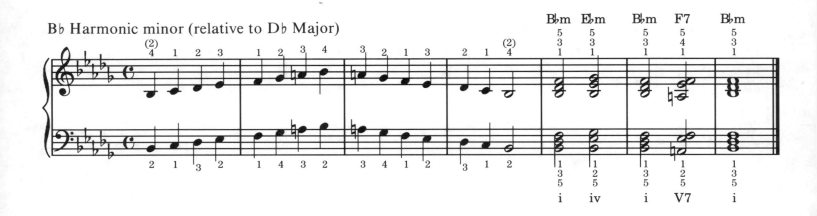

G♭ Major

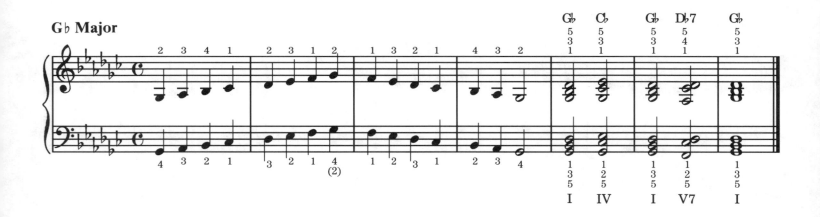

E♭ Harmonic minor (relative to G♭ Major)

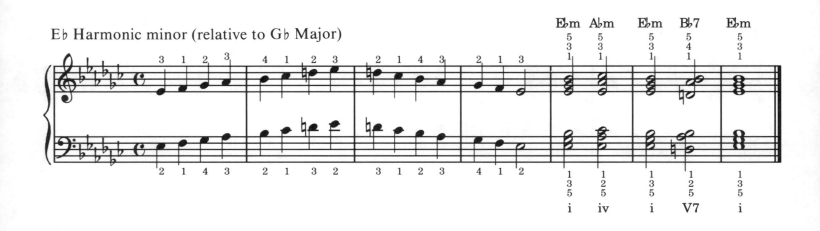

Review

1. Before each music symbol or word (Column 2), write the number of the correct definition (Column 1).

Column 1

1. Alla breve or "cut time" : may be used to indicate the **2/2** time signature

2. Gradually increase speed

3. Key signature 3 flats: indicates the key of E♭ Major or C minor

4. With expression

5. Key signature 3 sharps: indicates the key of A major or F♯ minor

6. Little by little

7. Very fast

8. Played on the same key of the keyboard, but having different names (F♯ and G♭ or C♯ and D♯)

9. Sixteenth note: receives one-fourth beat

10. In singing style

11. C major triad

12. Sixteenth rest: receives one-fourth beat of silence

13. C minor triad

14. Grace note: has no time value and is not counted as part of the rhythm; is played quickly before the principal note

15. C diminished triad

16. C augmented triad

17. Dotted eighth note: receives three-fourths of a beat, equal in value to three sixteenth notes

18. Slight accent mark

19. Very slow

20. Heavy accent mark

Column 2

_____

_____ *Accelerando*

_____

_____

_____

_____

_____

_____ *Poco a poco*

_____ *Adagio*

_____ *Espressivo*

_____

_____ *Presto*

_____ *Cantabile*

_____

_____

_____

_____

_____

_____ *Enharmonic tones*

_____

Music Dictionary

MUSICAL TERM	ABBREVIATION or SIGN	DEFINITION
Accelerando	*accel.*	Gradually increase speed
Accent mark	>	To make louder
Adagio		Slowly
Alla breve	¢	Cut time, with two beats to each measure; indicates time signature
Alla marcia		In march time
Allegretto		A little slower than allegro
Allegro		Fast, brisk
Andante		A walking tempo
Animato		Lively
A tempo		Return to the original tempo
Cantabile		In singing style
Chromatic scale		A series of twelve successive half steps; may begin or end on any note
Coda		An added ending
Con brio		With spirit
Crescendo	*cresc.* ◁	Gradually growing louder
Da capo al fine	*D.C. al fine*	Return to the beginning and play to the word *fine*
Dal segno al fine	*D.S. al fine*	Return to the sign (𝄋) and play to the word *fine*
Decrescendo	*decresc.* ▷	Gradually growing softer
Diminuendo	*dim.*	Gradually growing softer
Espressivo		With expression
Fermata	⌢•	Hold or pause
Forte	*f*	Loud
Fortissimo	*ff*	Very loud
Grace note		Played quickly before the principal note; has no time value and is not counted as part of the rhythm
Grazioso		Gracefully
Harmonic minor scale		Begins on the 6th tone of its related major scale (sharing the same key signature); the 7th tone is raised one-half step
Inverted triads		Triad with the root as the top note or middle note of the chord
Legato		Smooth and connected
Leger lines		Added lines and spaces above and below the music staff

Melodic minor scale .... Begins on the 6th tone of its related major scale (sharing the same key signature); 6th and 7th tones are raised one half step ascending, then lowered descending

Mezzo forte .... *mf* .... Moderately loud

Mezzo piano .... *mp* .... Moderately soft

Minor triad .... Consists of a root and the intervals of a minor 3rd (1½ steps) and a perfect 5th (3½ steps) above the root

Misterioso .... With an air of mystery

Moderato .... A moderate speed

Molto .... Much or very

Natural minor scale .... Begins on the 6th tone of its related major scale (sharing the same key signature)

Ottava .... *8va* .... When *8va* is placed OVER a note or group of notes, it means to play 8 keys (one octave) higher than written. When *8va* is placed UNDER the notes, it means to play 8 keys lower

Poco a poco .... Little by little

Pianissimo .... *pp* .... Very soft

Piano .... *p* .... Soft

Presto .... Very fast

Primary chords .... Triads built on the first, fourth and fifth notes (degrees) of the scale

Relative minor scale .... Scale related to the major scale through sharing the same key signature; begins on the 6th tone of the related major scale

Repeat sign .... To play over again

Ritardando .... *rit.* .... Gradually slowing down

Sforzando .... *sfz* .... With a sudden strong accent

Simile .... Continue the same

Slight accent .... – .... Sustain the tone slightly

Staccato .... *stacc.* .... Short, disconnected

Syncopation .... Shifting of the normal accent; a weak beat functioning as a strong beat

Ternary form .... A composition in three sections, A-B-A

Triplet .... A group of three notes played in the usual time value of two similar notes

Vivace .... With life, fast

Certificate

of

Accomplishment

This certifies that

_____

has completed

LESSONS
LEVEL FOUR
of the

David Carr Glover

METHOD for PIANO

HONOR

_____
(Teacher)

_____
(Date)